The Secret Life of the
Flying Squirrel

Laurence Pringle

Illustrated by
Kate Garchinsky

/\ ASTRA YOUNG READERS

AN IMPRINT OF ASTRA BOOKS FOR YOUNG READERS
New York

As a spring day ends in the woods, the sky grows dark.

Songbirds find safe places to sleep.

The sky grows darker. Bats flutter from their hiding places and begin to hunt for flying insects.

The sky grows darker. A small furry face with big black eyes and big ears appears at the entrance to a den in a tree. Volans, a southern flying squirrel, peeks out into the night.

During the day Volans had slept in a cozy nest. Sometimes
she woke up to groom her fur, licking with her tongue, combing
with her front claws. She even combed her long tail.

Her secret den is inside a tree hole that had once been made by a woodpecker. Her hideout isn't big, but Volans herself is small. Her body and tail combined are less than ten inches long. She weighs only a few ounces.

Volans climbs out onto a tree limb. She looks out at a forest she knows very well. She can see clearly with her big eyes. Flying squirrels are active at night (*nocturnal*) and have excellent night vision.

Although Volans is called a flying squirrel, she can't really fly. Bats are the only *mammals* that have wings and can fly. Bats can dive, soar, turn, and even hover in the air because they have wings and powerful muscles.

Volans has no wings. Instead, she has flaps of fur-covered skin on both sides of her body called *patagia* (pronounced "pa-tay-gee-ah"; one is called a *patagium*). They stretch from her wrists to her ankles. When she spreads them out, her body looks like an open sail or parachute. Using them, Volans can glide down from tall trees, make quick turns in the air, and land exactly where she aims.

Volans gets ready to glide. She crouches and looks out into the forest to choose a landing place. She turns her body and head from side to side. She bobs her head up and down. These looks, before she leaps, give her different views that help her pick a clear glide path.

Holding her legs close to her body, Volans leaps upward into the air, then starts to stretch her four legs out. This makes her patagia spread out. She begins to glide gently down through the night air.

Volans is a skilled glider. To turn left, she moves her left front leg so it is lower than her right leg. This tilt of her body makes her turn.

She also knows how to avoid a crash landing. She knows she must slow down as she nears her landing place. In an instant, she flips her tail straight up. Volans pulls her legs close to her body so her patagia fold up at her sides. She thrusts her rear legs and feet out ahead of her body, then the claws of all four feet grab onto tree bark. Her feet and legs absorb the jolt of her quick stop. With

Often, when Volans glides down to the bottom of a tree, she quickly scrambles high up its trunk, then glides to another tree. Then she climbs another tree and glides down, then another, and so on. From just one tall tree she may glide as far as three hundred feet. In this way, a flying squirrel can quickly travel a half mile or even farther through the woods.

Tonight, however, Volans simply wants to find some food from the tree where she landed. It is a shagbark hickory. Last fall she plucked hickory nuts from the tree's branches and twigs, then hid them under its bark. (A hidden secret food supply is called a *cache*. By her *instincts*, Volans knows how to gather, hide, and then later find her food caches.) Now she finds the hidden nuts, gnaws through their tough shells and eats the tasty food within.

Flying squirrels are *rodents*, related to mice and rats. All rodents have big front teeth that can be used to chew open nuts and seeds. Flying squirrels eat many nuts and seeds. They also eat berries and mushrooms. However, they sometimes eat bird eggs, mice, and the meat of dead animals. Since they eat both plant and animal food, they are *omnivores*.

Flying squirrels can scamper quickly on tree trunks and branches. However, traveling on the ground, on fallen leaves and among plants, rocks, and other obstacles, they can't move as fast. The forest floor can be a dangerous place for flying squirrels. They must stay alert for *predators*, including owls, foxes, and *feral* cats that hunt in the night.

Flying squirrels feel safer when they are off the ground. Some nights, Volans glides to a bird feeder. It is on top of a metal pole, near a house. Each day a family adds a fresh supply of sunflower seeds to the feeder. They enjoy seeing the songbirds that fly in to eat.

The people living in the house do not know that other, secret, seedeaters sometimes glide in at night—not just Volans but other flying squirrels she knows. One is her mate, who lives in a den near hers.

Tonight, Volans glides from tree to tree, exploring. She is *pregnant*. From feelings in her body, she knows she will soon give birth to squirrel pups. She wants a roomier hiding place.

In a dead tree she finds a hollow space that seems big enough and safe enough to be a nursery den. Volans stocks it with some hickory nuts and other food. She prepares a nest. She glides out into the night, again and again, and returns home with mouthfuls of leaves, grasses, mosses, and strips of bark from grapevines. With her teeth she shreds all of these materials and creates a soft, cozy bed.

On a rainy May morning, Volans gives birth to three pups. They are tiny, about the size of a large grape. They have no fur, just pink skin. Their eyes and ears are shut tight. They can't see or hear, though they can make little squeaking sounds.

They are helpless, but know how to do one thing. Soon each pup is nursing milk from their mother.

Before Volans gave birth, she was free to roam every night, gliding from tree to tree, hunting for food, and meeting other squirrels. Now she is a mother. She stays close to home, always ready to give her pups milk. With her tongue she licks their little bodies clean. She spreads her patagia, like warm blankets, over the pups.

They grow quickly. Soft, downy hair begins to cover parts of their skin. Their ears open. Their teeth start to grow. However, even when the pups are three weeks old their eyes have not yet opened. They still depend on Volans for all their food.

One evening the squirrel family awakens to scary sounds. The claws of a big animal scratch and scrape on tree bark just outside their den. Volans smells the odor of a dangerous predator. A raccoon has found the nursery den. It also smells something—little squirrels to eat.

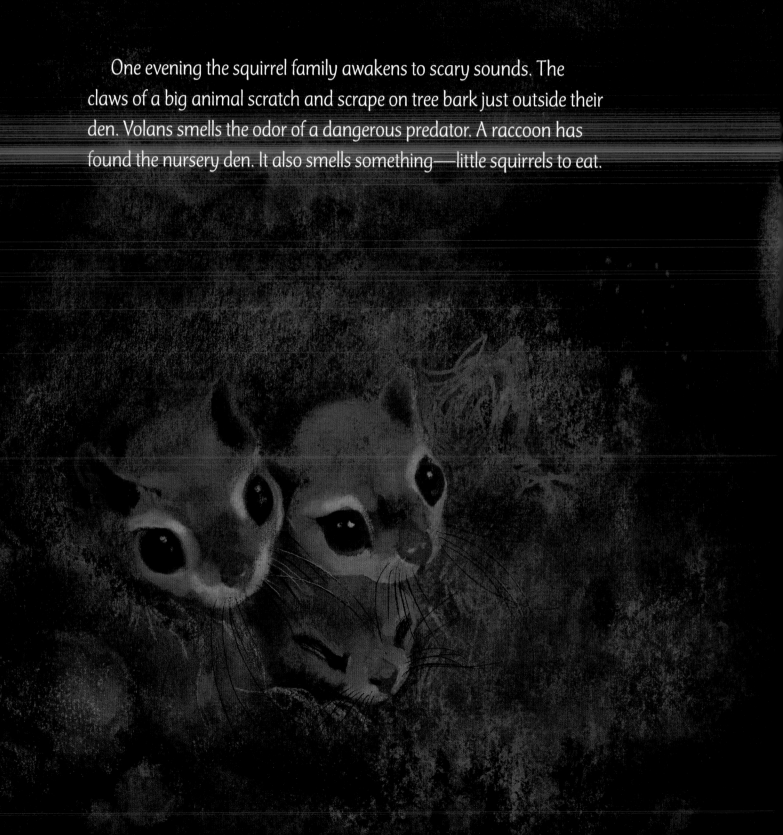

The den entrance is small, but the raccoon can still reach in with one front leg. Its paw and claws grope down into the den. It tries to grab a little squirrel.

Volans and her pups huddle in one corner, just out of reach. She rises up and gives the raccoon's paw a quick, sharp bite.

The raccoon quickly pulls its paw out of the den and hurries down the tree trunk, but Volans doesn't feel safe. Time to move! She knows the forest well. She knows of other hideouts.

With her nose, Volans flips one of her pups onto its back. She grabs its belly with her mouth. The pup curls up and wraps its body around part of her face. Carrying her pup, Volans glides into the night. She lands on the ground, scurries to another tree, climbs far up, and glides again. Soon she scrambles up the trunk of a tree she knows well. She pokes her head into the entrance of a den. It has a nest but no animal lives in it.

Volans leaves her pup in the nest, then hurries back to get another baby, and then her last one. At last, they are all together again, and safe. Volans is very tired. She and her pups snuggle and fall asleep in their new nest.

Thanks to their mother's milk, the pups grow fast. Their eyes open. They become more vocal. They chirp, cheep, chitter, and squeak. They chase and wrestle with one another. They play with old nut shells and other objects. Sometimes Volans needs a quiet time away from her *rambunctious* pups. She slips out of the den and rests on a nearby branch.

When the pups are about five weeks old, they start to venture out of their den. Before, they had little hints of the world beyond their nest. Now, at last, they can see, smell, and hear the wonders of the forest all around them.

The pups grow stronger every day. For a few more weeks they may still want to nurse milk, but they try berries and other food that Volans brings home. When the pups are seven weeks old, they start to become gliders. First, they glide short distances. They make mistakes. They bump into branches, or make bad landings, but they practice and get better. Soon the pups can leap from a tree and glide with confidence into the night.

Now all the delights, and dangers, of the forest in summer are theirs. Volans teaches them to look and listen for owls and other predators. She leads them to a feast of summer foods: beetles, moths, and other insects, spiders, slugs, berries, wild grapes, and seeds of many plants.

As summer slips away, so do Volans's pups. They are now able
to take care of themselves. Sometimes one may return to the family
nest to sleep. Volans also may meet one of her pups in the forest,
but her job as a mother is over.

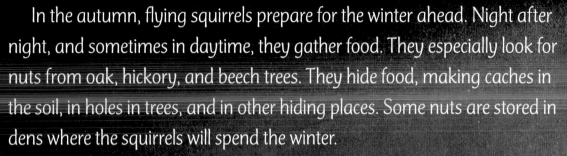

In the autumn, flying squirrels prepare for the winter ahead. Night after night, and sometimes in daytime, they gather food. They especially look for nuts from oak, hickory, and beech trees. They hide food, making caches in the soil, in holes in trees, and in other hiding places. Some nuts are stored in dens where the squirrels will spend the winter.

When winter comes, Volans joins a dozen other flying squirrels in a hollow space inside a tree. Her nestmates are young and old, one of her pups, aunts and uncles, maybe a grandparent, even strangers. They all cuddle together to keep warm. They sleep a lot, groom their fur, and sometimes go out in the wintry cold to fetch food.

Outside, a snowy wind blows. Inside, Volans feels warm and safe.

More About Flying Squirrels

In this book, the name Volans given to the mother squirrel comes from the species scientific name for the southern flying squirrel: *Glaucomys volans*. In Greek, *glaukos* means "silver or gray," and *mys* is "mouse." *Volans*, from Latin, means "flying." Southern flying squirrels are the smallest of all North American tree squirrels—smaller than the gray, red, and fox species—and the smallest of the three species of flying squirrels that live in North America. The southern and northern kinds were identified more than two centuries ago. In 2017, however, scientists named a third, separate species: Humboldt's flying squirrel. It lives in forests along the Pacific Coast, from British Columbia to Southern California.

Earth is home to about fifty species of flying squirrels. Most live in Southeast Asia. One of the biggest, the red flying squirrel, is about two feet long and can weigh more than six pounds. It lives in parts of China, Thailand, India, and the island of Sumatra. Japan has a species called the giant flying squirrel (weighing up to five pounds) and also the dwarf flying squirrel (weighing only about seven ounces).

Southern flying squirrels live as far south as some mountain ranges in Mexico and even in Guatemala and Honduras of Central America. In the US, they are concentrated in the East and Midwest, from Florida and eastern Texas to southern Vermont and Minnesota, and some of Ontario, Canada. The range of the northern flying squirrel is truly northern, mostly in Canada and Alaska, but includes New England and New York in the east, and parts of several Great Lakes states in the US. Some live in the mountain forests of North Carolina, Virginia, and Tennessee. In several northern states the two main species coexist.

Northern flying squirrels usually have one litter of young a year. The southern species usually has two litters in the warmest parts of its range, but only one in the coldest parts. In warmer climates, both of these species often make nests of twigs and leaves on tree branches in the summer. In colder climates, and in winter, they prefer more sheltered nests within tree trunks. As is true of many kinds of rodents, male flying squirrels do not help females raise young.

Scientific observations have revealed some fascinating details about flying squirrels and their adaptations to a nocturnal, gliding life. Slow-motion films of the squirrels in flight show that they do not use their tails to help steer. The tail's flat shape does help, however, as a surface area that adds "lift" to the spread-out patagia. Also, observers noticed that a squirrel, landing on the trunk or branch of a tree, usually scuttles quickly around to the opposite side. This behavior would help the squirrel escape from an owl, if one silently swooped after a gliding squirrel.

In autumn, flying squirrels sense the shortening of day length. This triggers their intense harvesting and hiding of food. On autumn nights they can be heard making tapping sounds in the woods, as they use their teeth or snouts to pound nuts into cracks and other secure places on tree bark. They do not hibernate, even in the extreme cold winters of their northern range. They do, however, spend much of winter in their shelters, and are especially inactive in the coldest weather. They rely on stored fat in their bodies and the nuts and other foods they have gathered.

Flying squirrels may be the most abundant tree squirrels in North America. However, thanks to their secretive nocturnal lives, they are seldom seen. Many people do not know these squirrels live nearby. They are surprised when a pet cat catches one and brings it home. Or, looking under a hickory tree, they find empty nutshells, each with a small circle chewed by a flying squirrel in order to remove the food within. (Bigger squirrels make bigger holes.) Some people discover they have flying squirrel neighbors when squirrels set up a nest in their house, usually in the attic. This can be a nuisance (sounds of scampering overhead) and destructive (when nest-building squirrels shred papers, clothing, and other items). The remedy is to livetrap and release the squirrels outside while also finding and blocking their entranceways to the house. With the problem solved, many people are delighted to have these creatures as neighbors.

Glossary

Cache: a hiding place for something valuable. The word can also describe an action, for example, "The squirrel cached many acorns and other nuts."

Feral: an animal that was once tame, or descended from domesticated animals, and lives in the wild.

Instincts: natural acts or behaviors of animals that they do without thinking or experience.

Mammals: warm-blooded animals with hair or fur that give birth to live young. Female mammals can feed their young with milk from mammary glands. Squirrels, bats, cows, dogs, and humans are all mammals.

Nocturnal: active at night.

Omnivore: an animal that eats both plants and animals.

Patagia: fur-covered membranes of skin that extend from the wrists to the rear ankles on each side of a flying squirrel. When spread out and stretched tight, the two patagiums act like a parachute, slowing the fall of the squirrel and enabling it to glide through the air for a hundred feet or more.

Predator: an animal that hunts and eats other animals.

Pregnant: having one or more unborn young developing within the body of a female mammal.

Rambunctious: behavior that may be loud, rowdy, unruly, unrestrained.

Rodent: a mammal with large front teeth that are good for gnawing open nuts and seeds. Rodents include mice, rats, squirrels, and beavers.

More Books About Flying Squirrels

Bishop, Nic. *The Fantastic Flying Squirrel*. New York: Collins, 2005.

Jango-Cohen, Judith. *Flying Squirrels*. Minneapolis, MN: Lerner, 2004.

Wells-Gosling, Nancy. *Flying Squirrels: Gliders in the Dark*. Washington, DC: Smithsonian Institution Press, 1985.

Zappa, Maria. *World's Weirdest Animals: Flying Squirrels*. Minneapolis, MN: Abdo Publishing, 2016.

Dedicated to all of nature that has deeply affected my life, first by giving a lonely, curious boy a sanctuary—the ponds, creeks, and forests of the Hopper Hills in Mendon, NY. Thanks for wildlife adventures in the Adirondack Mountains, Sonoran Desert, New Zealand, Costa Rica, and for nearly 50 years near my West Nyack home. Thank you, nature, for filling my life with wonder, mystery, and delight. —*LP*

For my steadfast friend and kindred spirit, Larry. I'm glad you liked my fox sketch. With love —*KG*

The author and illustrator thank Richard Essner, Jr., PhD, professor in the department of biological sciences at Southern Illinois University Edwardsville, for his careful review of the text and illustrations.

The illustrator would like to thank Michele Wellard at Philadelphia Metro Wildlife Center in Norristown, PA, for her assistance with valuable photo reference, and the Dimeler family for providing southern flying squirrel-watching opportunities at their home in Media, PA. Very special thanks to Tony Croasdale at Philadelphia Parks and Recreation, Blake Goll at Willistown Conservation Trust, and all the environmental educators in the world who chose to dedicate their lives to inspiring our planet's future wildlife stewards. You are so important.

Astra Young Readers
An imprint of Astra Books for Young Readers,
a division of Astra Publishing House
astrapublishinghouse.com
Printed in China

ISBN: 978-1-63592-529-6 (hc)
ISBN: 978-1-63592-548-7 (eBook)
Library of Congress Control Number: 2021925886

First edition
10 9 8 7 6 5 4 3 2 1

The text is set in Mercurius CT.
The illustrations are painted digitally in Procreate.